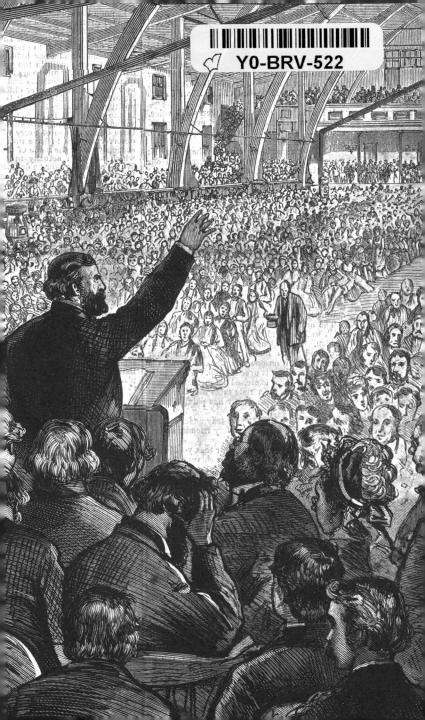

That Old-Time Religion

That Old-Time Religion

THE HUMOR, REVERENCE, AND JOY

OF AMERICAN RELIGION

IN AN EARLIER TIME,

WITH JUST A TOUCH

OF NOSTALGIA

Edited by Jan Gilmore
and Ginny Jacoby

HALLMARK EDITIONS

PRESENTED TO

Mom

by

Anne

Teacher.

'Tis the Old-Time Religion

This favorite hymn has a simple
—almost monotonous—melody.
But it captures the spirit of camp-meeting days
and the days of pioneering and hardship.
Even those who did not experience such things
can feel them in the rhythmic refrains
of this soulful song.

1. 'Tis the old - time re - lig - ion, 'Tis the old - time re - lig - ion

2. Makes me love ev - 'ry - bod - y, Makes me love ev - 'ry - bod - y,

3. It was good for Paul and Si - las, It was good for Paul and Si - las,

(Verse 1 for Chorus)

'Tis the old - time re - lig - ion, And it's good e - nough for me.

Makes me love ev - 'ry - bod - y, And it's good e - nough for me.

It was good for Paul and Si - las, And it's good e - nough for me.

Backwoods Preaching

*Religion in the frontier backwoods
presented preachers with some unusual challenges,
as captured in this selection
from* Bible in Pocket, Gun in Hand.

It was the almost total ignorance of religion in some parts of the backwoods that shocked and discouraged the ministers most. One of them told of approaching a man, busy on his small farm, and by way of attempting to lead him to an interest in a religious life, asked him if he did not "want to be a laborer for the Lord."

"No, thank you," the man replied, "I have a job." And he wiped the perspiration from his face, and set to work again without question or comment.

Preachers were thwarted in their work by many of the backwoods people's lack of a sufficient vocabulary to communicate with understanding on religion.

A traveling preacher told of examining a woman at her home on her beliefs, and asking if she had any religious convictions.

"Naw," she replied bluntly, "nor my ole man neither. He war tried for hog-stealin' once, but he warn't convicted."

A Presbyterian missionary arrived at a lonely cabin in a clearing, and hoping to find some fellow

6

member of his denomination, asked the woman of the cabin: "Are there any Presbyterians in this country?"

The woman, obviously assuming that the man, riding the dim trails through the woods, must be a hunter of animals like her husband, replied: "Wal, I just couldn't say for sure about that. These woods is full of most every kind of varmet, but I ain't paid much attention to 'em. You might take a look around there on the back side of the cabin where my husband keeps his varmet hides, and see if he's got any Presbyterian hides nailed up. If there's any Presbyterians in this country, he's . . . caught one by now."

Never on Sunday

In Papa Was a Preacher *Alyene Porter,*
a rural preacher's daughter,
recalls her father's determination
to make Sunday a day of rest.

Papa's first assignment in the new life was the serving of six rural churches. On horseback he traveled to the six points on his "circuit." Since that time . . . he has voiced the gospel to Texans in rural chapel, in small-town church, and in city temple.

From those first years he has obeyed the literal law

of his beliefs. In rearing eight children Papa has never found it necessary to buy on Sunday. Feed for his circuit-riding horse was bought on Saturday; gasoline for his car is still bought on Saturday. Even ice and milk for Sunday were delivered the night before. We usually kept a cow, but once when we were without one Papa opened a sleepy eye on Sunday morning to see the milk ordered for Saturday night being placed on the doorstep. He went to the telephone.

"Mrs. Brown," he kindly addressed the wife of the dairyman-farmer, "I'm sorry. We don't buy milk on Sunday."

"But Brother Porter," came her incredulous protest, "unfortunately the cows *give* milk on Sunday."

"Yes," sighed Papa in regretful tone, "unfortunately!"

The Great Awakening

The huge crowds attending marathon revivals brought into existence the "camp meeting."

The leader of the revival movement in Kentucky and Tennessee was James McGready, a Presbyterian minister.

McGready was a spark fallen into the tinder: at

a revival meeting in May 1797 a woman "was struck with deep conviction, and in a few days was filled with joy and peace in believing." The awakening had begun in Kentucky, and through the years 1798 and 1799 spread rapidly. Pinched spirits found relief through the wondrous ways of the revivals. To a four-day meeting held at McGready's church at Gasper River in July 1800, crowds came from such distances that it was necessary to provide accommodation for them. A suggestion was made that they should all camp on or near the meeting ground; thus the "camp meeting" came into existence.

A camp meeting in 1859.

Amazing Grace!
How Sweet the Sound!

*The story of John Newton's memorable hymn
is recalled by Billy Graham.*

It seems to me that "Amazing Grace" is really Newton's own testimony of his conversion and of his life as a Christian. He might have begun the hymn with the first stanza of another of his poems, "He Died for Me," but these words have somehow dropped out of use:

> In evil long I took delight,
>   Unawed by shame or fear,
> Till a new object struck my sight,
>   And stopped my wild career.

"God's grace" has been defined as "His undeserved favor." It was this grace that reached out to John Newton. When he learned that Christ loved him and had died for him, he was amazed. It was this grace which made him conscious that he was a sinner ("grace taught my heart to fear") and then assured him that his sins were forgiven ("grace my fears relieved"). So it is with all of us. We are all "great sinners" not only because of transgressions committed, but also because we fall short of God's standard for

*An old-time church choir leads the
Sunday morning singing.*

our lives. And this "amazing grace" is available to all of us.

As Christian believers we continue to experience God's undeserved love and favor throughout all of life. Every day He forgives our shortcomings, if we confess them. Every day He supplies all our needs.

They tell us that the last stanza of this song was not written by John Newton. But I think he would agree that it is a fitting climax to his testimony. After he—and we—have been in heaven for ten thousand years worshipping our Lord, we will still have endless time to sing of His amazing grace!

Amazing grace! how sweet the sound,
    That saved a wretch like me!
I once was lost, but now am found,
    Was blind, but now I see.

'Twas grace that taught my heart to fear,
    And grace my fears relieved;
How precious did that grace appear
    The hour I first believed!

Through many dangers, toils and snares,
    I have already come;
'Tis grace hath brought me safe thus far,
    And grace will lead me home.

When we've been there ten thousand years,
    Bright shining as the sun,
We've no less days to sing God's praise
    Than when we first begun.

yes, ten thou-
f the stoutest,
thing to with-

ger you are in:
and bottomless
are held over in
is provoked and
inst many of the
der thread, with
ng about it, and
d burn it asunder;
y Mediator, and
urself, nothing to
thing of your own,
e, nothing that you
u one moment.
re present, that yet
e. That God will ex-
, implies that he will

uld be dreadful to suf-
of Almighty God one
t to all eternity....
at is out of Christ, now
to come. The wrath of
ubtedly hanging over a
on: Let every one fly out

From Testimonies to Trains

*The one-room country church was the scene
of many a bitter tear as the men and women
of the farm shared their trials
and tribulations with one another.*

One day in 1903, a class meeting was in progress in a one-room country church. It lasted an hour, and about half the people who had attended the earlier Sunday school remained. The wallpapered sanctuary, with rag carpet on the pulpit platform and in the two aisles, was heated by two big wood and coal stoves, one against the north wall and the other exactly opposite inside the south aisle. There was no cloakroom so we stacked our heavy coats in empty pews. The big room was pleasantly filled with the odor of fresh stove polish that the fires heated and made to shine.

The meeting was conducted with great dignity by an old farmer who was also superintendent of the Sunday school. He quoted Bible verses now and then and generally spoke a few words of encouragement to the man or woman who had just stood up and given testimony. More women than men spoke up, but then as now there were more women in church. Farm women led lonelier lives, too, and they must have derived sound relief from speaking up. Often when

they had finished they sat do~~
vice was a lay activity, nc
there were vague and piou
ance.

What I most vividly reme.
ercises in mutual aid is the
faces of the men and women w
much weeping. They talked abc
and heaven. . . .

Religion was intensely person.
like [the] gospel songs, like the clas
toral care. Those earlier congregati
from revival meetings and from alta
max of Sunday worship. Conversion \
al experience and unreflective. The c
the Spirit moving him; he knew his
had been "washed in the blood of the La
not expected to explain the mystery.

Sermons of the time were highly emo
even from the educated clergy. They wer
ically barren; they were moralistic, pra
single sermon might bring in Noah's ark, Lc
and the sin of Sunday train excursions.

ten thousand times greater than it is,
sand times greater than the strength
sturdiest devil in hell, it would be no
stand or endure it. . . .

O sinner! Consider the fearful dan
it is a great furnace of wrath, a wide
pit, full of the fire of wrath, that you
the hand of that God, whose wrath
incensed as much against you, as ag
damned in hell. You hang by a sle
the flames of divine wrath flashi
ready every moment to singe it, ar
and you have no interest in a
nothing to lay hold of to save y
keep off the flames of wrath, no
nothing that you ever have don
can do, to induce God to spare y
Consider this, you that are h
remain in an unregenerate sta
ecute the fierceness of his ange
inflict wrath without any pity.
It is *everlasting* wrath. It w
fer this fierceness and wrath
moment; but you must suffer
Therefore, let every one th
awake and fly from the wrat
Almighty God is now undo
great part of this congregati

of Sodom: "Haste and escape for your lives, look not behind you, escape to the mountain, lest you be consumed."

Jonathan Edwards

Born and Reborn

*Brush arbor meetings were the scene
of more than prayers and testimonies,
as reflected in this selection
from* The Deacon Wore Spats *by John T. Stewart.*

I can recall brush arbor meetings under forest trees and torchlight, with wood chips in place of sawdust in the aisles, and the revivals ("protracted meetings" they were called), which were held every summer after the corn was laid by. . . .

Attending a brush arbor revival meant sitting on a bare plank without a back rest, fighting mosquitoes, and standing up every few minutes to let somebody in or out of the row. The congregation was constantly changing throughout the two or three hours—women took their crying babies out, men took themselves out. Men brought their buggy whips into the meeting and held them like a beggar's staff—if the tasseled whips were left in the dashboard sockets, they wouldn't be there when the meeting was over. Sometimes harnesses were slashed with a knife or a horse's tail left tied in a painful knot. Fist fights were frequent in the darkness under the trees. . . .

The last brush arbor meeting I attended was in the 1920s. . . . While our driver was cruising about trying to find a safe parking place, his car lights fell upon a

Brush arbor revivals were a lot livelier than regular church. This drawing shows an arbor meeting in progress.

young couple locked in a most compromising embrace on the back seat of a car. Our driver remarked, "Sometimes I think more souls are born than reborn from these brush arbor meetings."

19

Julia Ward Howe

The Battle Hymn of the Republic

*One of the traditional examples of American spirit,
Julia Ward Howe's work is an expression
of the evangelical fervor of the 19th century.
This is from the original version of the poem
as it first appeared in*
The Atlantic Monthly, *February 1862.*

Mine eyes have seen the glory of the coming of the
    Lord:
He is trampling out the vintage where the grapes of
    wrath are stored;
He hath loosed the fateful lightning of His terrible
    swift sword:
                His truth is marching on.

I have seen Him in the watch-fires of a hundred
    circling camps;
They have builded Him an altar in the evening dews
    and damps;
I can read His righteous sentence by the dim and flar-
    ing lamps:
                His day is marching on.

I have read a fiery gospel writ in burnished rows of
 steel:
"As ye deal with my contemners, so with you my
 grace shall deal;
Let the Hero, born of woman, crush the serpent with
 his heel,
      Since God is marching on."

He has sounded forth the trumpet that shall never
 call retreat;
He is sifting out the hearts of men before His judg-
 ment-seat:
Oh, be swift, my soul, to answer Him! be jubilant,
 my feet!
      Our God is marching on.

In the beauty of the lilies Christ was born across the
 sea,
With a glory in his bosom that transfigures you and
 me:
As he died to make men holy, let us die to make men
 free,
      While God is marching on.

Just the Crows and the Preachers

The circuit riders of the frontier days
went everywhere. They rode through blizzards,
snowstorms, and cloudbursts,
prompting an old folk saying that at such times
"nobody was out but crows and Methodist preachers."

In an old record there is the story of Richmond Nolley, a circuit rider who had traveled several days without seeing any sign of human habitation. Late in the afternoon in a remote section of Mississippi, he came upon a fresh wagontrack. On the search for anything that had a soul, he followed it, and came upon the emigrant family just as it had pitched on the ground of the future home. The man was unlimbering his team, and the wife was busy around the fire. "What!" exclaimed the settler, upon hearing the salutation of the visitor, and taking a glance at his unmistakable appearance, "have you found me already? Another Methodist preacher! I quit Virginia to get out of reach of them; went to a new settlement in Georgia, and thought to have a long whet, but they got my wife and daughter into the Church. Then, in this late purchase—Choctaw Corner—I found a piece of good land, and was sure I would have some

23

peace of the preachers; and here is one before my wagon is unloaded."

Nolley gave him small comfort. "My friend, if you go to heaven, you'll find Methodist preachers there; and if to hell, I am afraid you'll find some there; and you see how it is in this world. So you had better make terms with us, and be at peace."

24   *Neither rain nor snow nor gloom of night kept the Methodist circuit rider from his rounds.*

Acrobatic Preaching

*Billy Sunday, early-day evangelist, was known
for putting body and soul into his sermons.*

People understand with their eyes as well as with
their ears; and Billy Sunday preached to both. The
intensity of his physical exertions certainly enhanced
the effect of the preacher's earnestness. No actor on
the dramatic stage worked harder. Such passion as
dominated Sunday cannot be simulated; it is the soul
pouring itself out.

Some of the platform activities of Sunday made
spectators gasp. He raced to and fro across the platform. Like a jackknife he fairly doubled up in em-
phasis. One hand smote the other. His foot stamped
the floor as if to destroy it. Once I saw him bring his
clenched fist down so hard on the seat of a chair that I
feared the blood would flow and the bones be broken.
No posture was too extreme for this restless gymnast.
Yet it all seemed natural. Like his speech, it was an
integral part of the man. Every muscle of his body
preached in accord with his voice. . . .

Sunday was a physical sermon. In a unique sense
he glorified God with his body. . . . When in a sermon
he alluded to the man who acts no better than a four-
footed brute, Sunday was for an instant down on all
fours on the platform and you saw that brute. As he

pictured a man praying he sank to his knees for a single moment. When he talked of the deathbed penitent as a man waiting to be pumped full of embalming fluid, he could not help going through the motions of pumping in the fluid. He remarked that deathbed repentance was "burning the candle of life in the service of the devil, and then blowing the smoke in God's face." The last phrase was accompanied by "pfouff!" In a dramatic description of the marathon, he pictured the athlete falling prostrate at the goal and—thud!—there lay the evangelist prone on the platform. Only a skilled baseball player, with a long drill in sliding to bases, could fling himself to the floor without serious injury. On many occasions he took off his coat and talked in his shirt sleeves. It seemed impossible for him to stand up behind the pulpit and talk only with his mouth.

The fact is, Sunday was a born actor. He knew how to portray truth by a vocal personality. When he described the traveler playing with a pearl at sea, he tossed an imaginary gem into the air so that the spectators held their breath lest the ship lurch and the jewel be lost.

Evangelist Billy Sunday demonstrates the body-and-soul enthusiasm he put into his lively sermons.

Swing Low, Sweet Chariot

*This spiritual was born among the Negroes
of the South and captures their personal sorrows
and hopes. It depicts the journey they hoped to take
from the burdens of slavery to the promised land.*

Southern Negroes at a revival meeting.

Slow.

Swing low, sweet char - i - ot, Com-ing for to car-ry me

home; Swing low, sweet char-i-ot, Com-ing for to car-ry me home.

home; . . . .

FINE.

1. I looked o - ver Jor - dan, and what did I see,
2. If you get there be - fore I do,
3. I'm some - times up, I'm some - times down,

Com-ing for to car-ry me home? A band of an - gels
Com-ing for to car-ry me home; Tell all my friends I'm
Com-ing for to car-ry me home; But still my soul feels

D. C.

com-ing af - ter me, Com-ing for to car - ry me home.
com - ing too, Com-ing for to car - ry me home.
heav-en-ly bound, Com-ing for to car - ry me home.

29

A Backslider's Reward

James Knox in Sunday's Children *writes of the woe
that befell a "sinner" who forsook
church attendance on Sunday.*

It is difficult on drowsy summer Sundays not to look
out of the church windows to watch the magic mo-
notony of its motion and listen to the quiet song it
sings. Even Father, in his pulpit, would often stare
dreamily out of the window toward the stream and
the fields that lay beyond.

On one such Sunday, when Father was in the
midst of his sermon, we noticed how often he glanced
that way. Soon he began edging toward the window,
intently interested in something outside. It wasn't
long before everyone who was sitting near the row of
windows was looking, too, and we saw a man walk-
ing slowly along swinging a stick and stooping every
few paces to pick up a stone to throw in the brook.
We thought the noise of the plop was bothering Fa
ther, but that wasn't it. A few yards behind the walk-
ing man walked a goat. Every time the man stooped
down, the goat paused and lowered its head. The situ-
ation was full of suspense. Father's preaching went
on without a break, while he wondered and we all
wondered when or if the issue would be joined. The
goat timed his charge to the split-second—seeming to

30

know with some sixth sense when the man would bend down. The man flew through the air with a startled cry, the goat, its mission accomplished, ran happily across the field with its back feet kicking in the air and Father stamped his foot and slapped his leg in the way he did when he was very pleased. "Another backslider has learned," Father announced to the congregation, "that the safest place to be on Sunday morning is in the church."

Sinners First

D. L. Moody was an evangelist of fire and fervor whose crusades swept England, Canada and the U. S. in the late 1800s.

When Mr. Moody was on a journey, in the western part of Massachusetts, he called on a brother in the ministry on Saturday, to spend the Sabbath with him. He offered to preach, but his friend objected on account of his congregation having got into a habit of going out before the meeting was closed. "If that is all, I must and will stop and preach for you," was Moody's reply. When Mr. Moody had opened the meeting and named his text, he looked around on the assembly and said:—"My hearers, I am going to speak to two sorts of folks to-day—saints and sinners!

Sinners! I am going to give you your portion first, and would have you give good attention." When he had preached to them as long as he thought best, he paused and said, "There, sinners, I have done with you now; you may take your hats and go out of the meeting house as soon as you please." But all tarried and heard him through.

32   *Famed evangelist Dwight L. Moody preaching at the Hippodrome around 1875.*

Donation Parties

*Donation parties were held whenever a circuit rider
came to town. Here a circuit rider's new bride
relates her reaction to her first donation party.*

William went out to put up his red-headed horse, and
I drew a chair before the shelf containing the bread
tray, the dishpan, pot and skillets, and stared at them
with horror and amazement. Why had William not
mentioned this matter of cooking? I had never cooked
anything but cakes and icings in my whole life! I was
preparing to weep when a knock sounded upon the
door and immediately a large, fair woman entered.
She wore the most extraordinary teacup bonnet on
her huge head that was tied somewhere in the creases
of her doubled chin with black ribbons. And, on a
blue plate, she was carrying a stack of green-apple
pies nearly a foot high. Catching sight of the half-
distilled tears in my eyes as I arose to meet her, she
set the pies down, clasped me in her arms and whis-
pered with motherly tenderness: "I know how you
feel, child; it's the way all brides feel when they first
realize what they have done, and all they've done to
theirselves. But 'tain't so bad; you'll come down to it
in less 'an a week; and you mustn't cry now, with all
the folks comin' in. They won't understand."

She pointed through the open door and I turned in

the shelter of her arms to see down the road a strand
of people ascending the hill, dressed like fancy beads,
each behind the other, and each bearing something in
her hands or on his shoulders—and William standing at the gate to welcome them.

"Who are they?" I asked in astonishment.

"It's a donation party. I come on ahead to warn
you. Them's the members of the Redwine, Fellow-
ship and Macedonia churches, bringin' things to cele-

34   *Grateful townspeople helped their preachers with*
"donation parties." The gifts ranged from bedquilts
to homecured tobacco.

brate your weddin'. I'm Glory White, wife of one of the stewards at Redwine, and we air powerful glad to have you. So you mustn't cry till the folk air all gone, or they'll think you ain't satisfied, which won't do your husband any good."

. . . Everyone called me "Sister Thompson" and laid a "donation" on the table in passing. I was not aware at the time of their importance, but as William only received two hundred and forty-five dollars for his salary that year we should have starved but for an occasional donation party. . . . Upon this occasion they ranged from bedquilts to hams and sides of bacon; from jam and watermelon rind preserves to flour, meal and chair tidies. One old lady brought a package of Simmons' Liver Regulator, and Brother Billy Fleming contributed a long twist of "dog shank"—a homecured tobacco. The older women spread the viands for the "infare," as the wedding dinner was called . . . and we stood about it to eat amid shouts and laughter and an exchange of wit as good natured as it was horrifying to bridal ears.

The Coming of
the Circuit Rider

The coming of a circuit rider to a settlement
was always an exciting occasion—especially
when he was one of the controversial Methodists
as illustrated in this excerpt from The Circuit Rider
by Edward Eggleston.

"Hello the house!" cried the stranger. . . .

"Hello, stranger, howdy?" said Colonel Wheeler, advancing with caution, but without much cordiality. He would not commit himself to a welcome too rashly; strangers needed inspection. "Light, won't you? . . . A preacher, I reckon, sir?"

"Yes, sir, I'm a Methodist preacher, and I heard that your wife was a member of the Methodist Church, and that you were very friendly; so I came round this way to see if you wouldn't open your doors for preaching. I have one or two vacant days on my round, and thought maybe I might as well take Hissawachee Bottom into the circuit, if I didn't find anything to prevent."

By this time the Colonel and his guest had reached the door, and the former only said, "Well, sir, let's go in, and see what the old woman says. I don't agree with you Methodists about everything, but I do think that you are doing good, and so I don't allow anybody to say anything against circuit riders without taking it up."

Mrs. Wheeler, a dignified woman, with a placidly religious face—a countenance in which scruples are balanced by evenness of temperament—was at the moment engaged in dipping yarn into a blue dye that stood in a great iron kettle by the fire. She made haste to wash and dry her hands, that she might have a "good, old-fashioned Methodist shake-hands" with Brother Magruder, "the first Methodist preacher she had seen since she left Pittsburg."

Colonel Wheeler readily assented that Mr. Magruder should preach in his house. Methodists had just the same rights in a free country that other people had. He "reckoned the Hissawachee settlement didn't belong to one man, and he had fit aginst the King of England in his time, and was jist as ready to fight aginst the King of Hissawachee Bottom." The Colonel almost relaxed his stubborn lips into a smile when he said this. Besides, he proceeded, his wife was a Methodist; and she had a right to be, if she chose. He was friendly to religion himself, though he wasn't a professor. If his wife didn't want to wear rings or artificials, it was money in his pocket, and nobody had a right to object. Colonel Wheeler plumed himself before the new preacher upon his general friendliness toward religion, and really thought it might be set down on the credit side of that account in which he imagined some angelic bookkeeper entered all his transactions. He felt in his own mind "middlin' certain," as he would have told you, that "betwixt the prayin' for he got from *such* a wife as his, and his own gineral friendliness to the preachers and the Methodis' meetings, he would be saved at the last, *somehow* or *nother*."

The Great Life

Even in the days of old-time religion, it was difficult for a preacher to satisfy his congregation.

"If the minister's hair is white, he is too old. If he is young, he lacks experience. If he has ten children, he has too many; if he has none, he should have, to set a good example. If his wife sings in the choir, she is presuming; if she doesn't, she isn't in sympathy with his work. If he reads his sermons, he is a bore; if he preaches extemporaneously, he is shallow. If he spends much time in his study, he isn't a good mixer; if he gets about a great deal, he ought to be home making better preparation for Sunday. If he calls on a poor family, he is playing to the grandstand; if he calls on the rich, he is aristocratic. It's a great life— if you don't weaken."

Church "Sessions"

The importance and power of church "sessions"
as governing bodies and arbitrators is set forth
in this selection from Protestants and Pioneers.

The session could admonish, suspend, or exclude the offenders from the sacraments. The session also admitted members into the church, initiated action to promote its spiritual welfare, and appointed the delegates to the higher judicatories of the church. In addition, the session was required to keep accurate records of its own proceedings as well as of the baptisms, marriages, new members, deaths, persons admitted to the communion, and those dismissed or dropped. . . .

Two ways were provided for bringing cases of assumed misconduct to trial. Either various individuals brought charges or the matter came to the attention of the session through "common fame." The session then summoned the necessary witnesses as well as the member concerned to its next meeting when it questioned the witnesses before the accused. The latter had the right to examine and to refute their testimony. Unlike the secular courts, the sessions banned professional counsel. Cases tried before the church sessions typically involved such diverse charges as consenting to illegal marriage, excessive drinking, questionable business practices, refusing to commune because of difficulties with another person, publicly accusing others before taking steps as prescribed by the church, attending or allowing one's children to attend places of "vain amusement," imprudent and unchristian conduct, and obstinate refusal to honor the church.

The following random extracts from the Records of the Forks of Elkhorn Baptist Church will illustrate the hearings (only excerpts of the minutes for any single day are given):

2nd Saturday in Sepr. [1801] the Church met and after Divine Worship proceeded to business.

Charges brought against Bro, Shackleford for various reports circulating respecting his Immoral conduct Gaming etc & Brethn, J Price & Haydon is appointed to Cite him to Meeting to Morrow morning.

Thos. Hickman came forward confessed his fault & was restored. . . .

Bro. Zacheriah Ross is Excluded from this Church
for drinking too an Excess & for disobeying the
call of the Church.

Br. Thomas Hickman is Excluded from this Church
for drinking to an Excess & for fighting.

*The church "session" was a powerful governing body
that influenced not only the religious activities of
church members, but their secular activities as well.*

The Minister's Bonus

*The church social filled the preacher's stomach
and lined his pockets.*

The church mouse did not achieve his legendary reputation for leanness from mere accident. He was no doubt the inhabitant of a country church in the days of our grandfathers when he sometimes ran a poor second to the minister.

The underpaid, and often unpaid, ministers to the souls of our rural forefathers were often reduced to a polite form of begging and few of their families rose above genteel undernourishment. Their parishioners had no illusion about how much food and clothing the eighty or a hundred dollars a year, an average salary, would buy. The customary supplement to this starvation wage was the church social, given as a benefit for the preacher and his family.

Church socials were held on the lawn of the church on summer evenings. Members of the church donated cake, platters of fried chicken, canned preserves, fruit, and other delicacies of the season which were served at plank tables laid on wooden sawhorses. Food was served family style and the usual cost of a church social meal was twenty-five cents for all you could eat. Ten cents was charged for children, who usually ate twice as much as their elders. Society leaders of the community presided at the cake table, where the work was easy and where they got a chance to compare the baking skill of their neighbors. The preacher's wife and the lesser members of the congregation washed dishes and served the hot food from a brick stove or kerosene range set up for the evening under a canvas. It was a gala time for the children of the community, who could play on this rare occasion when neither Sunday school nor public school cast a shadow on their spirits.

The swain who squired a girl at a church social dinner was a marked man, for this was understood by all as an open and public declaration of serious intentions. There was no trifling with tradition.

The minister's family was richer by twenty-five or thirty dollars, everybody had a good time, and every housewife gathered up enough leftovers to feed her family the next day, a phenomenon of the fish and loaves sort that was very mysterious and wonderful.

Testimony and the Vision

In Erskine Caldwell's Deep South *a young man who has "enjoyed sin for a season" feels particularly well equipped to preach to others about its pitfalls.*

I tell you, I was just about the biggest sinner than anybody else was around up there where I used to live. Some of the folks who heard me confessing my sins at the revival said I was making up most of it out of my head. Good people would think that. But sinful people like I was didn't doubt the truth when they heard me tell it.

But getting converted and confessing my sins and then seeing that vision sure changed me from real bad to real good in a hurry. And I ain't done none of them things since all that happened and I can look anybody straight in the face and say how good I am since. But I ain't sorry about my sins after confessing. I figure I know more about sin than most folks and that's why I can preach against it so good now.

I told my wife right after confessing and seeing the vision that I was a changed man and that she wouldn't have no cause to think no more that I was like I used to be. She didn't say much of anything right away, because she knowed all about my . . . habits, and I reckon she was just waiting to find out if I was telling the truth or another big lie again.

The way I came to find out about this place to preach at here was when I told the preacher back up there at home what the vision said for me to do. He said I'd had the vision just at the very right time, because he'd heard about a new church down here that was an offshoot of another one and it needed a preacher. After I'd told him all about the vision I saw, he said he was sure this was the exact place where God wanted me to come to. He told me there wasn't enough members down here so far to pay me a full-time living but that one of the members promised he could help make up for it by getting me a part-time job in a lumber yard. That suited me because I've been used to heavy work all my life. . . .

One good member told me not long ago he'd never heard a real expert before tell about sinful things the way I do. Sometimes I get to thinking what if I was still back up there where I used to be and hadn't got converted and my soul saved and then hadn't seen the vision to top it off.

When I get to thinking like that, it won't be long till I get down on my knees and thank the Lord for getting me the real religion and seeing the vision. . . . That sure was a lucky thing for me. Besides all the souls I'm saving for Jesus, I get three full days work at the lumber yard and can keep half of all the money put in the collection plates on Sunday. . . .

The Cane Ridge Camp Meeting

*The Cane Ridge camp meeting, August 6, 1801,
is thought to be the largest revival ever held.
In* They Gathered at the River
*Bernard A. Weisberger tells of the huge crowds
and dynamic preaching
for which the meeting became legendary.*

The preachers congregated at Cane Ridge had never seen anything like it. Some of them guessed that 20,000 people were on hand. One put it as high as 25,000, a fantastic total in view of the fact that in 1800 there were not more than a quarter of a million people in Kentucky, so scattered that Lexington, the state's largest city, had only 1795 residents. But all the figures were somewhat imprecise. . . .

Whatever the numbers, there was abundant confusion. Technically, the meeting was Presbyterian, but Baptist and Methodist preachers had come to join in, and there was room for them. Even a Boanerges, a "son of thunder," could not reach a mob of such dimensions alone, so several preaching stands were set up. At eleven on Saturday morning two Presbyterian ministers were holding forth in the meetinghouse. One hundred and fifty yards away, another

Presbyterian brought the good news of salvation to a crowd around his feet. Off in another direction a Methodist had an audience pressing close to him. Nearby was a knot of Negroes, one of them loudly exhorting the others. Besides the preachers, some of the worshipers, undistracted by the competition, were telling private gatherings of *their* experiences. One account said there were as many as 300 of these laymen "testifying." The ministers were handing out lead tokens to admit people to the communion, with no questions asked about denomination, and on Saturday morning alone 750 were distributed.

The crowds were without form and void. They collected, listened, shouted "Amen!" and "Hallelujah!" and then broke up and drifted away to find friends, or refreshment, or more preaching. The din must have been enormous; the "stricken" were groaning, the preachers shouted, crowds of the unredeemed contributed a number of hecklers, children unquestionably cried, and horses stamped their hoofs and whinnied. There was a sound like the "roar of Niagara." At night, when campfires threw grotesque shadows of trees across the scene, the whole crowd seemed "agitated as if by a storm." It rained and thundered, to make things more spectacularly impressive. Those without tents got drenched, but the work went on.

Even if there had been only these things—the

A camp meeting in southern New York in 1836.

shouts, the wagons, the murmurous, plastic crowds, surging in the half darkness under the rain-beaten branches, Cane Ridge would have burned itself into the memories of men who were there. . . .

Many stories of unusual transports of holy joy and anguish were undoubtedly stretched. Some came from supporters of the revivals, accepting all that they heard in the firm belief that "with God nothing shall be impossible." Others were planted by opponents, who were trying to underscore the element of caricature in the meetings. But there was good evidence that the spirit often overcame the believers in one way or another. The Reverend Archibald Alexander, in a dignified Connecticut church publication, said that "falling down" created a problem at first during the Cane Ridge affair, but later on grew so familiar that it disturbed nobody. A Kentucky gentleman wrote to his brother in Virginia that he had seen a meeting where hundreds lay prostrate on the ground, and no mere uneducated riffraff or hysterical children, either, but "the learned pastor, the steady patriot, and the obedient son . . . the honorable matron and the virtuous maiden crying, Jesus, thou son of the most high God, have mercy on us."

The revival should have brought unanimous rejoicing in the religious world. The "unchurched" Western territory, the cause of so much despair and so many missionary societies, now seemed to be ablaze with piety. Thousands were listening eagerly to the gospel and crowding to enroll themselves among the saved. It was easy to thank the Lord enthusiastically for such undeserved, but welcome, mercies.

Praise the Lord and Raise the Roof

Many old-time preachers measured faith in terms of volume.

When I was a boy certain preachers had standard phrases they relied on to provoke cries of "Amen," and any evangelist who didn't "raise the roof" was not invited back another year. The old-time revivalists loved spontaneous encouragement. Today a minister would feel heckled if his congregation interpolated loud shouts of agreement during his discourse.

I remember an elderly . . . bishop who worked for an hour and a half to thaw out a prewar congregation. He tried all his tricks but met only stony silence. Exasperated, finally, he interrupted his sermon to ask, "Are those bald heads I see down there or tombstones?"

No one answered.

"You, brother," he said, pointing to a man in an aisle seat, "have you a voice?"

The man nodded but did not speak.

"Then use it, man, use it," the bishop begged. "How does the Lord know you are a Christian unless you shout out the glory?"

His listener merely looked uncomfortable.

"Praise the Lord!" shouted the bishop. Even that drew no reaction. Again he pointed down the aisle.

"Can you say 'Praise the Lord'?"

"Why, of course."

"Then say it, man, say it."

The man said it.

"You whisper!" the bishop roared. "Is that all you think of the Lord? Can't you shout? Come, now, follow me. Praise the Lord!"

This time there was a faint echo.

"That's better. Shout it now, louder."

The man shouted.

"Hallelujah!" cried the bishop. "Everyone in the auditorium, now, repeat after me, and use your lungs! Hallelujah!"

The reaction was half-hearted but promising.

"That's the spirit. Again, with all your might. Hallelujah!"

"Hallelujah!" came the answer.

"Now, after me: Praise the Lord!"

"Praise the Lord!"

"Now once more: Amen!"

"Amen!" This time the answer was tumultuous.

The bishop mopped his brow and smiled. "That's better," he said. "I was afraid for a moment I was addressing heathen."

Selling Out for the Lord

*The great expense of early revivals was met
in unique ways as related in this story about
the evangelistic team of D. L. Moody and Ira Sankey.*

The money to meet [the expenses of the meetings] came for the most part from private donations, though local corporations sometimes gave.

Another method of raising money was to hold a special dedication ceremony at the tabernacle prior to the revival to which admittance was by special invitation only. Printed on the invitation was the statement, "The person using this ticket is expected to make a freewill offering to the Lord of not less than one dollar toward meeting the expense of this sacred enterprise; or more as God may have given ability."

. . . Still another way in which money was raised was to sell the materials used in building or renovating the meeting halls after the revival. A notice in the Philadelphia newspapers announcing the need

DWIGHT L. MOODY   IRA D. SANKEY

for an additional $9000 to meet the expenses [of the Philadelphia meeting] said, "At the close of the meetings the flooring and other lumber fittings, and also the furniture will be sold at public auction for the account of this fund.' An account of this auction in the Washington *Evening Star* noted that a sofa and chair used by Moody and Sankey in their "retiring room" at the tabernacle "brought prices far above their value." Then "the towels used by the evangelists were taken up. Mr. Shaw handled them in a reverential manner, announcing the great importance attached to them as relics and asked someone to start them. '50¢' cried one of the auditors. '$1' said another.

Two, three, four, and finally five dollars apiece was bid for the two used by Mr. Moody and knocked down to a Mr. Johnstone. 'Now,' said the auctioneer, 'I have the towels used by Mr. Sankey. . . .' " Mr. Shaw also managed to auction off the Bible rest, the crimson plush on the pulpit, and the chairs the evangelists had sat upon on the platform.

Sunday-Go-to-Meeting

A Sunday morning ritual is recalled in
The Good Old Days—An Invitation to Memory
by R. J. McGinnis.

On Sunday we put on our best clothes and went to church. This was an ordeal for the entire family, for "Sunday-go-to-meeting" clothes were no joke, especially to us kids. We went barefooted all week and when we put on shoes our feet burned like fire all during the trip to and from church, and during the services. Mother put on her corset, which cut her freedom to near zero, but made her stand very straight and dignified. Father got into his broadcloth suit, which he'd had since his wedding. It was fine for winter, but a veritable Turkish bath in summer.

All our skirts and dresses were starched as stiff as sheet iron, and everybody walked around like knights in armor. We were cautioned to "keep nice and clean" for it was a disgrace to appear at church with even a ruffle mussed.

To us children Sunday church was genuine torture, and it was not much better for the older people. We endured it because we were told to; the oldsters because they thought it was good to suffer a little.

The church was in the village at the crossroads, under a spread of trees. There were hitching racks in the rear, near the little cemetery. Father tied up the horse there, throwing a blanket over him if it were cold; in summer he tried to find a shady place.

We saw everybody we knew at church. The men liked to arrive a little early, gathering in knots outside under the trees and talking crops. The women eyed the new dresses and talked cooking and canning. We stood around miserably, not being allowed to shout or muss our clothes.

The sermon was too long for most everybody, but the choir sang well, and the notes from the pump organ were sweet. The word of God was good for men and women who had been isolated in fields and lonely farmhouses.

In summer the ride home was dusty and hot, in winter cold and bleak. But when we got home there was a big Sunday dinner, and the blessed relief of getting in our everyday clothes again.

*Church was a meeting place for members of the
community. Everyone came—the children because
their parents made them, the adults because "they
thought it was good to suffer a little."*

The Female Pied Piper

Aimee Semple (Sister) McPherson was a woman evangelist whose dramatic style gained worldwide attention during the Roaring Twenties.

Visiting her parents' Ingersoll farmhouse, Aimee, now known as Sister McPherson, explained her desire to return to religious work. Her delighted mother agreed to take charge of the children, and Aimee set out for Kitchener, where a big tent revival meeting was being held.

After the first meeting she offered her services to the campaign leaders, who assigned her to wash the dishes. Later she graduated to playing the piano where, according to her own account, she "hit every key from top to bottom." So useful did Sister McPherson become that she was asked by the evangelist's wife to help in the London (Ontario) campaign. She even painted a banner: COME TO THE GREAT CAMP MEETING.

In August, 1915, Aimee was invited to conduct Revival Services at a Pentecostal mission, where her husband assisted her, and here her world-wide ministry began.

Disappointed with her first small congregation inside the tiny church, Sister McPherson, chair in hand, marched to the main corner of town, where the sight of a beautiful woman preaching from a street corner naturally drew a crowd of men and women. Then, like the Pied Piper of old, Aimee led them into church.

Not until the end of the first week did she have the courage to take up her first collection, which amounted to sixty-five dollars. By this time, her revival meetings had grown to such proportions that they had to be held on a large lawn. With the collection money, Aimee purchased a second-hand tent, but it proved to be badly mildewed and full of holes.

Undaunted, Sister McPherson, assisted by some of the faithful, worked hours to patch it. Finally the tent was raised into position, gaily camouflaged with hand-painted texts. In the middle of her first sermon a high wind caused it to sag dangerously. The congregation had no time to panic, for the lady evangelist screamed, "In the name of the Lord, I command you to stay there 'til the meeting is over!"

"Believe it or not," Aimee recalls, "that tent caught on a protruding nail and stayed!"

The Old Rugged Cross

*The immortal hymn by the Rev. George Bennard
has captivated the hearts of generations of Christians.
In simple but expressive words and melody,
a fundamental belief in the power of the Cross
is conveyed. The song has sustained millions
on life's journey and has become
the most widely known hymn in America.*

1. On a hill far a-way stood an old rugged cross, The   emblem of
2. Oh, that old rugged cross, so   despised by the world, Has a wondrous at -
3. In the old rugged cross, stained with blood so di-vine, A   won - drous
4. To the old rugged cross I will ev - er be true, Its   shame and re -

suf - f'ring and shame; And I love that old cross where the dear - est and best
trac - tion for me;   For the dear Lamb of God left His glo - ry a - bove
beau - ty I   see;   For 'twas on that old cross Je - sus suf - fered and died
proach glad-ly   bear; Then He'll call me some day to my home far a - way,

For a world of lost sin-ners was slain. So I'll cher-ish the old rug-ged

To   bear it   to dark Cal - va - ry.

To   par - don and sanc-ti - fy me.

Where His glo - ry for - ev - er I'll share.   cross,   the

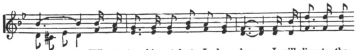

cross, ... Till my tro-phies at last I lay down; I will cling to the

old rug-ged cross,

old rug-ged cross, ... And exchange it some day for   a   crown.

cross,   the old rugged cross,

Set in Intertype Walbaum, a light, open typeface designed by Justus Erich Walbaum (1768-1839). Headlines and titles set by Boston Typefoundry in a version of University Text, an outlined Victorian Gothic frequently used in early prayer books. Printed on Hallmark Eggshell Book paper. Designed by Susan Howey.